FIRST SOLOS
FOR THE
TROMBONE
(OR BARITONE)
PLAYER

TRANSCRIBED BY
HENRY CHARLES SMITH

G. SCHIRMER, Inc.

DISTRIBUTED BY

HAL•LEONARD®
CORPORATION
7777 W. BLUEMOUND RD. P.O. BOX 13819 MILWAUKEE, WI 53213

CONTENTS

		Piano	Trombone
BACH, JOHANN SEBASTIAN	Jesu, meine Freude (Jesus, my joy)	16	5
	O Haupt voll Blut und Wunden (O Sacred Head Now Wounded)	17	6
	Was Gott tut, das ist wohlgetan (What God does, only that is right)	18	6
DONAUDY, STEFANO	Amor s'apprende (Love is understood)	4	2
	Sento nel core (I feel it in my heart)	2	2
EICHMAN, ARLEN D.	Serial Piece	39	10
GIORDANI, GIUSEPPE	Caro mio ben (Dearest, believe)	6	3
HELLER, ALFRED	Sweet Trip	37	10
MENDELSSOHN, FELIX	If With All Your Hearts (from *Elijah*)	10	4
	Theme from Italian Symphony (No. 4)	21	7
	Theme from Reformation Symphony (No. 5)	24	7
PERGOLESI, GIOVANNI BATTISTA	Nina	8	4
SCHUBERT, FRANZ	Ave Maria	12	5
	Litany	14	5
	Theme from Symphony No. 5	19	6
WAGENSEIL, GEORG C.	Concerto for Trombone (Second movement)	28	8

FOREWORD

This book is dedicated to my favorite young trombone-baritone player, my son Chuck, and to all young players. I hope that it will help them to play with a beautiful musical line and a rich sound and that it will lead them on to explore the vast treasures of great music.

I have transcribed many vocal pieces for this collection because young players need most of all to use their wind effectively in order to make sustained melodic lines and to "sing" with their instruments. I have deliberately kept the ranges, key signatures, and technical demands of the pieces simple enough so that young soloists and their accompanists can readily handle them. I hope that advanced students and professionals will also find this book a welcome addition to the repertoire and that the themes from symphonies, the Wagenseil concerto, and the novelties, as well as the songs and arias, will motivate students and their teachers to seek constantly for additional music which is appropriate and adaptable for the trombone and baritone horn.

H.C.S.

First Solos for the Trombone (or Baritone) Player

Transcribed by Henry Charles Smith

Sento nel core
(I feel it in my heart)

Stefano Donaudy
(1879-1925)

Amor s'apprende

(Love is understood)

Stefano Donaudy

Allegretto
Canon for 2 players

Caro mio ben

(Dearest, believe)

Giuseppe Giordani
(1744 - 1798)

Larghetto

Nina

Giovanni Battista Pergolesi
(1710 - 1736)

If With All Your Hearts

from: Elijah

Felix Mendelssohn
(1809 - 1847)

Ave Maria

Franz Schubert
(1797 - 1828)

Litany

Franz Schubert

Jesu, meine Freude

(Jesus, my joy)

Johann Sebastian Bach
(1685–1750)

Broad and sustained

O Haupt voll Blut und Wunden

(O Sacred Head Now Wounded)

Johann Sebastian Bach

Broad and sustained

Was Gott tut, das ist wohlgetan

(What God does, only that is right)

Johann Sebastian Bach

Theme from Symphony No.5

Franz Schubert

Trombone

FIRST SOLOS

FOR THE

TROMBONE
(OR BARITONE)
PLAYER

TRANSCRIBED BY

HENRY CHARLES SMITH

G. SCHIRMER, Inc.

DISTRIBUTED BY

HAL•LEONARD®
CORPORATION
7777 W. BLUEMOUND RD. P.O. BOX 13819 MILWAUKEE, WI 53213

CONTENTS

		Piano	Trombone
BACH, JOHANN SEBASTIAN . . .	Jesu, meine Freude (Jesus, my joy) .	16	5
	O Haupt voll Blut und Wunden (O Sacred Head Now Wounded) . .	17	6
	Was Gott tut, das ist wohlgetan (What God does, only that is right) . . .	18	6
DONAUDY, STEFANO	Amor s'apprende (Love is understood)	4	2
	Sento nel core (I feel it in my heart) .	2	2
EICHMAN, ARLEN D.	Serial Piece	39	10
GIORDANI, GIUSEPPE	Caro mio bèn (Dearest, believe) . .	6	3
HELLER, ALFRED	Sweet Trip	37	10
MENDELSSOHN, FELIX	If With All Your Hearts (from *Elijah*)	10	4
	Theme from Italian Symphony (No. 4)	21	7
	Theme from Reformation Symphony (No. 5)	24	7
PERGOLESI, GIOVANNI BATTISTA .	Nina	8	4
SCHUBERT, FRANZ	Ave Maria	12	5
	Litany	14	5
	Theme from Symphony No. 5 . . .	19	6
WAGENSEIL, GEORG C.	Concerto for Trombone (Second movement)	28	8

FOREWORD

This book is dedicated to my favorite young trombone-baritone player, my son Chuck, and to all young players. I hope that it will help them to play with a beautiful musical line and a rich sound and that it will lead them on to explore the vast treasures of great music.

I have transcribed many vocal pieces for this collection because young players need most of all to use their wind effectively in order to make sustained melodic lines and to "sing" with their instruments. I have deliberately kept the ranges, key signatures, and technical demands of the pieces simple enough so that young soloists and their accompanists can readily handle them. I hope that advanced students and professionals will also find this book a welcome addition to the repertoire and that the themes from symphonies, the Wagenseil concerto, and the novelties, as well as the songs and arias, will motivate students and their teachers to seek constantly for additional music which is appropriate and adaptable for the trombone and baritone horn.

H.C.S.

First Solos for the Trombone (or Baritone) Player

Transcribed by Henry Charles Smith

TROMBONE

Sento nel core
(I feel it in my heart)

Stefano Donaudy
(1879 - 1925)

Amor s'apprende
(Love is understood)

Stefano Donaudy

Caro mio ben
(Dearest, believe)

Giuseppe Giordani
(1744-1798)

Nina

TROMBONE

Giovanni Battista Pergolesi
(1710 - 1736)

Andantino

If With All Your Hearts

from: Elijah

Felix Mendelssohn
(1809 - 1847)

Andante con moto

Ave Maria

TROMBONE

Franz Schubert
(1797~1828)

Litany

Franz Schubert

Jesu, meine Freude

(Jesus, my joy)

Johann Sebastian Bach
(1685~1750)

O Haupt voll Blut und Wunden

(O Sacred Head Now Wounded)

TROMBONE

Johann Sebastian Bach

Was Gott tut, das ist wohlgetan

(What God does, only that is right)

Johann Sebastian Bach

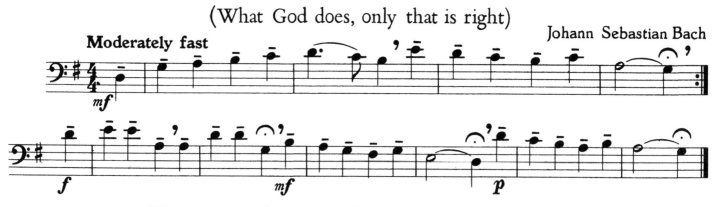

Theme from Symphony No. 5

Franz Schubert

Theme from Italian Symphony (No. 4)

TROMBONE

Felix Mendelssohn

Theme from Reformation Symphony (No. 5)

Felix Mendelssohn

Concerto for Trombone
(Second movement)

Georg C. Wagenseil
(1715 - 1777)

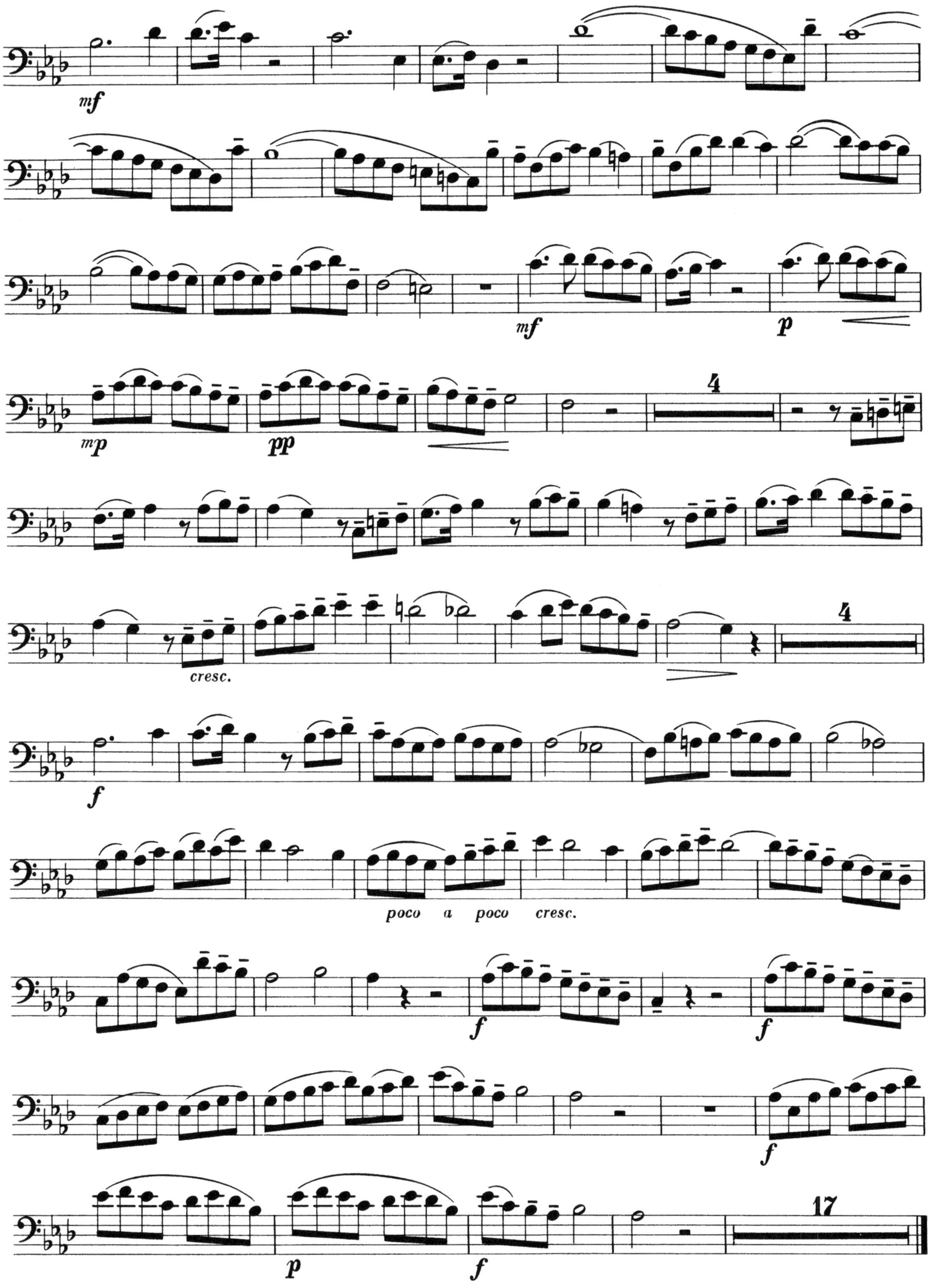
mf
mf
p
mp
pp
4
cresc.
4
f
poco a poco cresc.
f
f
f
p
f
17

Sweet Trip

TROMBONE

Alfred Heller

Serial Piece

Arlen D. Eichman

Theme from Italian Symphony (No.4)

Felix Mendelssohn

Theme from Reformation Symphony (No.5)

Felix Mendelssohn

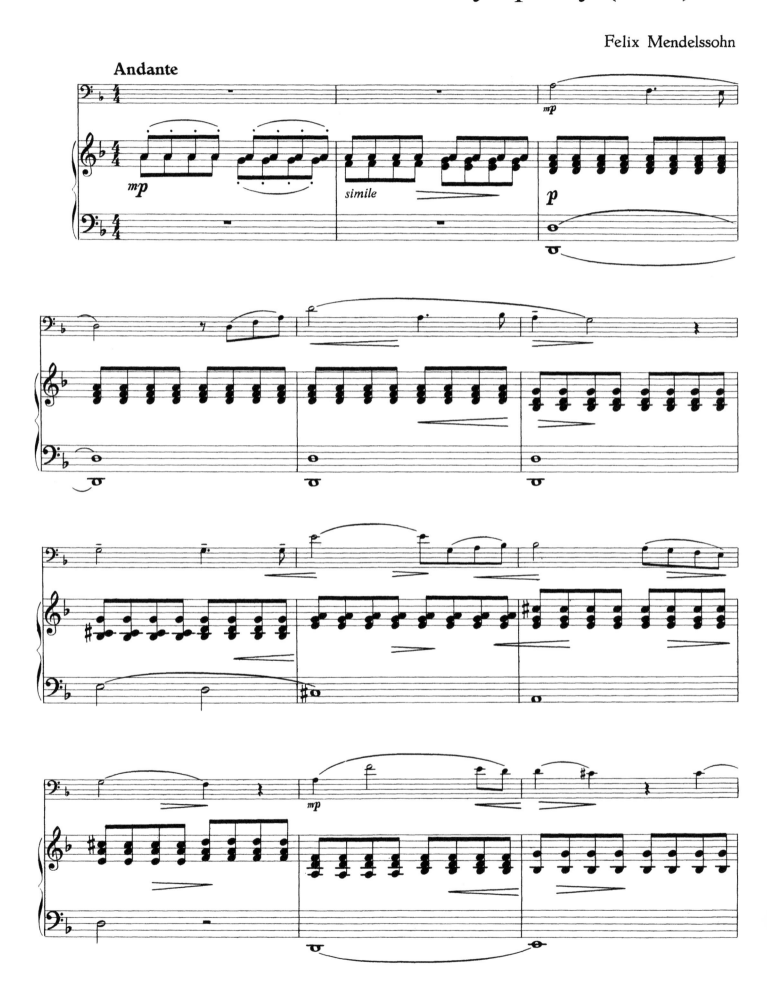

Concerto for Trombone

(Second movement)

Georg C. Wagenseil
(1715 - 1777)

poco   a   poco   cresc.

poco   a   poco   cresc.

Sweet Trip

Alfred Heller

Serial Piece

Arlen D. Eichman

Moderato

poco a poco crescendo

poco a poco crescendo

poco a poco decresc.

molto rit.

Allegro marcato

ritard.

molto ritard.

mf

p

Moderato

meno mosso

p

pp